W9-BCQ-905

JUNIOR
BIOGRAPHIES

CHINA ANNE McCLAIN

ACTRESS, SINGER, AND SONGWRITER

Kristen Rajczak Nelson

Enslow Publishing
101 W. 23rd Street
Suite 240
New York, NY 10011
USA

enslow.com

WORDS TO KNOW

ad-libbing To make up words to say based loosely on a script.

audition To try out for a part in a show.

comedienne A female comedian.

imitate To copy.

influence To have an effect on.

nominate To select as one possibility for a position or award.

premiere To give the first showing of.

prodigy A very talented child.

reprise To play the same part again.

CONTENTS

R0453301328

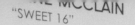

CHINA ANNE MCCLAIN
"SWEET 16"

BANNERS.COM

STICKERSBANNERS.COM

STICKERSBANNERS.COM

CHINA ANNE MCCLAIN
"SWEET 16"

STICKERSBANNERS.COM

ST

CHINA ANNE MCCLAIN
"SWEET 16"

CHINA ANNE MCCLAIN
"SWEET 16"

STICK

Teen star China Anne McClain started singing and acting when she was very young. She has been featured in big movies like *Grown Ups* and has become a popular comedienne from her time on the Disney Channel show *A.N.T. Farm*. Today, she's hard at work making movies and music she loves.

BORN TO BE A STAR

When China Anne was born on August 25, 1998, her family was already working in show business. Her father, Michael McClain, has worked as a singer, songwriter, and music producer for many years. Her mother, Shontell McClain, has also worked as a singer and songwriter. She has two older sisters named Sierra and Lauryn and a younger brother named

FUN FACT

China Anne began homeschooling in fourth grade to make it easier to pursue her career.

Gabriel, all of whom have worked singing or acting. China Anne's parents have run a production company called Gabesworld Music (named after Gabriel) since 2006.

It was China Anne's voice that first got her noticed. When she was five years old, she met a friend of her father's and sang him a song

Young China Anne had a flair for the dramatic from a very young age. Here she is in 2005.

China Anne Says:
"**Wherever my life is gonna go, I'll just let the wind carry me. I haven't really set out a path yet, but I'm walking it right now, so we'll see where I end up!**"

from the movie *Spy Kids* that she loved. He told director Rob Hardy about China Anne, knowing he needed a little girl to sing in his movie *The Gospel*. China Anne **auditioned**—and got the part! She played Alexis, a young singer in the choir. Her sisters were also part of the movie, which came out in 2005 when China Anne was only seven years old. It was just the beginning for China Anne, who says, "I loved it and realized I wanted to do it for the rest of my life."

The McClain sisters, Sierra Aylina, Lauryn Alisa, and China Anne (*left to right*), pose with brother Gabriel on the red carpet in 2007.

CHAPTER 2
MOVING ON UP

China Anne was born near Atlanta, Georgia. In 2006, she met famous Atlanta-based entertainer Tyler Perry. He cast her in his sitcom *Tyler Perry's House of Payne*, a show about a large family all living in one house together. As Jazmine Payne, China Anne became a familiar face in households across America. In fact, *House of Payne* was the longest-running sitcom to feature a mostly African American cast when it ended in 2012. Perry also cast China Anne and both her sisters in *Daddy's Little Girls* in 2007. Their characters were even named after the girls themselves!

China Anne Says:
"Mr. Perry has been a big influence in my life. He has also impacted many other people with the amazing messages involved in his plays and movies."

ON THE SILVER SCREEN

While she was on *House of Payne*, China Anne did

Tyler Perry's House of Payne was centered around a multi-generational family living in Atlanta, Georgia.

other acting work, too. She was a guest on many shows, such as *NCIS* and *Jimmy Kimmel Live*.

In 2010, China Anne played Charlotte McKenzie, Chris Rock's daughter, in the movie *Grown Ups*. She reprised her role in *Grown Ups 2* in 2013. "I definitely learned a lot about ad-libbing," China Anne says about working with comedy greats like Rock and Adam

Tyler Perry (*left*) took young China Anne and her sisters under his wing and helped her get her start in Hollywood.

Sandler. "Same thing with Tyler Perry—it's nothing but ad-libbing."

These early jobs helped China Anne develop her talent and prepared her for the next step in her career.

FUN FACT

China Anne and her family moved to Los Angeles, California, in 2011.

China Anne got to work with (*from left to right*) Chris Rock, Maya Rudolph, David Spade, Kevin James, and Adam Sandler in *Grown Ups*.

When China Anne first auditioned for Tyler Perry, she also auditioned for Disney. Though she didn't get the part, Disney didn't forget her. She had guest roles on *Hannah Montana*, *Jonas*, and *Wizards of Waverly Place*, as well as taking part in Disney Web videos. Seeing her talent, Disney worked hard to create a show just for her.

ON THE *A.N.T. FARM*

In 2011, *A.N.T. Farm* premiered on the Disney Channel. China Anne played Chyna Parks, an eleven-year-old music

A.N.T. Farm took place in San Francisco and followed a group of talented teens.

prodigy who starts going to high school as part of the Advanced Natural Talents program. The show allowed China Anne to show off her musical talents as well as her skills as a **comedienne**. She even performed the theme song to the show! *A.N.T. Farm* was a hit. She acknowledges that it can be hard on young performers to have so much attention. But she has turned to someone who had a similar path and has remained true to herself: "Selena [Gomez] is my role model," China Anne told the *New York Times*. "I'm never going to disrespect myself—never."

Even though *A.N.T. Farm* ended in 2014, China Anne continued with Disney and starred in *How to Build a Better Boy* that same year.

In 2014, the NAACP awarded China Anne with an Image Award for her work as a young African American actress. She was **nominated** again in 2015, proof that her performances were having an impact.

China Anne Says:

"**Chyna really doesn't care what the high schoolers say or what they think about her. She says, 'Move out of my way, I'm going to make my big entrance.'**"

Selena Gomez helped guide China Anne as she became more famous. Selena had also started on the Disney Channel and then began a music career.

FUN FACT

The president of entertainment for the Disney Channel, Gary Marsh, told the *New York Times* that China Anne is "probably the most talented comedian we have encountered in 10 years."

In 2015, she began working on *Descendants: Wicked World,* voicing the daughter of the evil Dr. Facilier from *The Princess and the Frog.*

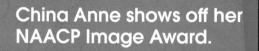

China Anne shows off her NAACP Image Award.

CHAPTER 4
MAKING MUSIC

China Anne showed off her singing talent in *The Gospel* and on Disney shows, including *A.N.T. Farm*. In 2014, she won a reality show called *Sing Your Face Off* that put celebrities against one another as they imitated the look and sound of famous singers. But she didn't set out to be a solo artist. China Anne wanted to sing with her sisters, Sierra and Lauryn, as they had grown up doing.

The three McClain sisters were signed by Hollywood Records in 2012. Together, they're called McClain. They've studied artists like Beyoncé and Michael Jackson for inspiration. They opened for boy group Big Time Rush in 2012, too. McClain has recorded numerous songs, including "Rise," the 2013 anthem for the Disney Friends for Change organization and featured song on the sound track for the Disney nature movie *Chimpanzee*.

The McClain sisters are more than actresses. They are also musicians and singers who enjoy performing together.

The McClain sisters have been working together on their music, but they're also hard at work on their YouTube channel! They make funny videos with their brother Gabriel and give advice to fans. China Anna has more than 1.5 million Twitter followers and is very active on Facebook and Instagram, too.

FUN FACT
China Anne plays guitar, bass, piano, and violin. She also played trumpet, French horn, drums, and harmonica on *A.N.T. Farm*.

China Anne Says:
"I started singing with my sisters and after *A.N.T. Farm* I have to go back to where I started."

China Anne loves posting photos with fans on social media!

The future looks bright for China Anne and her sisters.

The future looks bright for China Anne as an actress and musician. In 2016, she starred in her first thriller, *Brother's Blood.* In 2017, she continued voicing Freddie in Disney's *Descendants 2.* For such a young star, China Anne McClain seems determined to follow her dreams both alongside her family and on her own.

1998 China Anne is born on August 25 in Georgia.

2005 China Anne stars in *The Gospel*.

2006 China Anne starts to work on *House of Payne*.

2007 China Anne and her sisters are featured in *Daddy's Little Girls*.

2009 China Anne makes a guest appearance on *Hannah Montana*.

June 2011 *A.N.T. Farm* premieres.

2012 McClain signs with Hollywood Records.

2014 China Anne stars in *How to Build a Better Boy*; China Anne wins Outstanding Performance in a Youth/Children (Series or Special) at the NAACP Image Awards.

2015 China Anne sings on the sound track to and does voice acting for *Descendants: Wicked World*.

2016 China Anne signs on to play the role of Uma, Ursula's daughter, in *Descendants 2.*

BOOKS

Diver, Lucas. *Zendaya: Disney Channel Actress.* Minneapolis, MN: ABDO Kids, 2015.

Lassieur, Allison. *Astronaut Mae Jemison.* Minneapolis, MN: Lerner Publications, 2017.

Plowden, Martha Ward. *Famous Firsts of Women of Color.* Gretna, LA: Pelican Publishing Company, 2016.

WEBSITES

A.N.T Farm: Disney Channel

disneychannel.disney.com/ant-farm
Play games and watch videos with your favorites from *A.N.T. Farm*.

PBS Kids

pbskids.org/games/music/
Play fun games to learn about music.

Index

Published in 2017 by Enslow Publishing, LLC.
101 W. 23rd Street, Suite 240, New York, NY 10011

Copyright © 2017 by Enslow Publishing, LLC.

All rights reserved.

No part of this book may be reproduced by any means without the written permission of the publisher.

Library of Congress Cataloging-in-Publication Data:

Names: Rajczak Nelson, Kristen, author.
Title: China Anne McClain : actress, singer, and songwriter / Kristen Rajczak Nelson.
Description: New York, NY : Enslow Publishing, 2017. | Series: Junior biographies | Includes bibliographical references and index.
Identifiers: LCCN 2016020274| ISBN 9780766081864 (library bound) | ISBN 9780766081840 (pbk.) | ISBN 9780766081857 (6-pack)
Subjects: LCSH: McClain, China Anne—Juvenile literature. | Actresses—United States—Biography—Juvenile literature. | Women singers—United States—Biography—Juvenile literature. | Women musicians—United States—Biography—Juvenile literature. | African Americans—Biography—Juvenile literature.
Classification: LCC PN2287.M135 R35 2016 | DDC 791.4302/8092 [B] —dc23
LC record available at https://lccn.loc.gov/2016020274

Printed in China

To Our Readers: We have done our best to make sure all websites in this book were active and appropriate when we went to press. However, the author and the publisher have no control over and assume no liability for the material available on those websites or on any websites they may link to. Any comments or suggestions can be sent by email to customerservice@enslow.com.

Photo Credits: Cover, p. 1 Frazer Harrison/Getty Images; p. 4 Earl Gibson III/WireImage/Getty Images; p. 6 Moses Robinson/WireImage/Getty Images; p. 7 ZUMA Press, Inc./Alamy Stock Photo; p. 9 Alfeo Dixon/© TBS/Courtesy Everett Collection; p. 10 Vince Bucci/Getty Images; p. 11 Photos 12/Alamy Stock Photo; p. 12 Bob D'Amico/© Disney Channel/Courtesy Everett Collection; p. 14 Michael Loccisano/Getty Images; p. 15 Frederick M. Brown/Getty Images; pp. 17, 19 Robin Marchant/Getty Images; p. 20 Gregg DeGuire/WireImage/Getty Images; back cover, interior pages (curves graphic) Alena Kazlouskaya/Shutterstock.com; interior pages (reflections) liangpv/DigitalVision Vectors/Getty Images.